The Will of the People

T0056397

The Will of the People

A Modern Myth

Albert Weale

polity

First published in 2018 by Polity Press
Reprinted 2018, 2019 (twice)

Polity Press
65 Bridge Street
Cambridge CB2 1UR, UK

Polity Press
101 Station Landing
Suite 300
Medford, MA 02155, USA

ISBN-13: 978-1-5095-3326-8
ISBN-13: 978-1-5095-3327-5 (pb)

A catalogue record for this book is available from the British Library.

Library of Congress Cataloging-in-Publication Data

Names: Weale, Albert, Author.
Title: The will of the people : a modern myth / Albert Weale.
Description: Cambridge, UK : Medford, MA, USA : Polity Press, 2018. |
   Includes bibliographical references and index.
Identifiers: LCCN 2018019546 (print) | LCCN 2018034951 (ebook) | ISBN
   9781509533299 (Epub) | ISBN 9781509533268 | ISBN 9781509533275 (pb)
Subjects: LCSH: General will. | Democracy. | Political participation. |
   Common good.
Classification: LCC JC328.2 (ebook) | LCC JC328.2 .W42 2018 (print) | DDC
   321.8—DC23
LC record available at
https://clicktime.symantec.com/3QzXRDZt5bPTzypdfinnwLV6H2?u=https%3A%
2F%2Flccn.loc.gov%2F2018019546

Typeset in 12.5 on 15pt Adobe Garamond by Servis Filmsetting Ltd, Stockport, Cheshire
Printed and bound in the United States by LSC Communications

For further information on Polity, visit our website:
politybooks.com

Table of Contents

Acknowledgements   vi
Preface   viii

1 In the Grip of a Myth   1
2 Nostalgic Myths   15
3 What Is a People?   30
4 Majority Willing?   46
5 The Mythical Sovereign   67
6 On Being Outnumbered   81
7 Democracy without Myth   95
8 The Ethics of Responsibility   112

Notes and Sources   117

Acknowledgements

This book was written in a hurry and I prevailed upon the following people to read an earlier draft when they had good reason for doing other and more pleasurable activities. I should like to thank each and every one of them for their comments, criticisms and support. These people are Richard Bellamy, Sarah Birch, Roger Butler, Robert Field, Bob Goodin, Kasim Khorasanee, Des King, Jan King, Jeff King, Rudolf Klein, Cécile Laborde, Michael Lane, Pam Leadbetter, Joni Lovenduski, Iain McLean, Ted Marmor, Cas Mudde, Jack Nagel, Ian O'Flynn, Onora O'Neill, Katie Petty-Saphon, Jason Poole and Alan Ware.

Included in this group is a number of people who are not professional political scientists but took on the burden of telling me whether or not I was making sense outside of narrow specialist circles. I will not pick them out by name; they know who they are. But I am particularly grateful to them – not less than to my professional colleagues.

I thank the board of Polity for responding so positively to my suggestion that a book on the will of the people was timely. Originally the project arose from an almost casual enquiry on my part to David Held, whose abilities as a publisher are only matched by his skills as an analyst and commentator on politics and the global order. John Thompson kept me on the straight and narrow, always reminding me that inner conviction was no substitute for cogency of argument. Manuela Tecusan assiduously copy-edited the typescript to improve its clarity.

Jan Harris, as always, restored my sanity during the obsessive work of writing. She reinforced the sense that the argument needed to be advanced and allowed space in our lives, so that it might be written. What more could one ask?

Preface

This book arose from one specific incident in British politics. On 3 November 2016 the High Court gave its judgement in the *Miller* case. At issue was the question of whether the UK government needed parliamentary approval to trigger the process by which the United Kingdom would leave the European Union. The government argued that it did not need such approval. The three judges ruled that it did. On its front pages the following day, the Brexit-supporting press attacked both the verdict and the judges who had made it. 'The judges versus the people' exclaimed the *Daily Telegraph*. 'Enemies of the people' pronounced the *Daily Mail* in chorus, adding for good measure that one of the judges was an 'openly gay' former Olympic fencer. (The *Mail* did not make clear whether it was being gay, being a fencer, or being both that made the judge an enemy of the people.)

These responses were bad enough. To make matters worse, no cabinet minister, not even the Secretary of State for Justice, was prepared to explain and defend publicly the role of the courts in judging constitutional controversies. Here was a matter that the government itself had agreed was rightly a matter for the courts. In England, legally contesting the constitutional right of the government to act by executive decree goes back at least as far as the seventeenth century. Indeed, it is not hard to see that the government itself had an interest in resolving the uncertainty about its constitutional powers in such an important matter. And yet responsible ministers in the government remained silent. I had never thought that a government in the United Kingdom would undermine the rule of law and the constitution of the country it governed. I was wrong.

Yet I should not have been surprised. Theresa May had already said at the Conservative Party conference the previous month that those who argued that initiating the process for leaving the

European Union could only be triggered after agreement in both Houses of Parliament were not standing up for democracy but trying to subvert it. For her, the referendum of June 2016 had expressed the will of the people and it was not the place of parliament to undermine that will. You need to take a deep breath before you even attempt to get your mind around the steps of this argument. It begins by equating the will of the people with the outcome of the referendum. It goes on to equate government policy with the referendum result. It ends up by equating government policy with the will of the people. In consequence, parliament becomes the enemy of democracy and has to be replaced with government by executive decree. And all this in the name of the will of the people! As a citizen of a democratic country, you know you are in trouble when a political party – any political party – claims to embody the will of the people. One people; one will; one-party state.

How could the idea of the will of the people so shape political decision-making about the most important matter of policy that the United Kingdom has faced in decades? One answer is that those who talk about the will of the people

are confusing democratic government with populist government. Populists think that government
policy should be decided by the people, who
should directly mandate governments to do its
will, without any need for parliamentary debate
or opposition. Around the world, populist political parties and movements – both on the left and
on the right – are mobilizing around the claim
that, if the people governed directly, all would
be well.

David Hume once said that the errors in reli-
gion were dangerous, but those in philosophy
only ridiculous. This book suggests that errors in
political philosophy can also be dangerous. The
will of the people is an idea drawn from political philosophy that has now become a modern
myth. It fosters the populist error that democracy
means the direct determination of government
policy by the people. Paradoxical as it might
seem, that view all too often has the effect of put-
ting more power into the hands of the executive.
When parties in government purport to speak for
the will of the people, they can manipulate politics to their own ends. When the idea of the will
of the people is used to silence dissent about an
important political choice, then a fundamental

principle of constitutional democracy – that democracy is institutionalized debate in which competing views are expressed within a set of rules – has been lost. Any pervasive myth is dangerous in a democracy; the myth of the will of the people is particularly dangerous.

I have tried to write this book for the general reader. It relies on academic research, some of which is highly technical or specialist. Indeed, I sometimes wonder how much of the further reaches of that research I understand myself. But the basic ideas are not obscure and can be understood by anyone who cares about the correct use of language, enjoys reading about history and likes doing a sudoku puzzle. I hope I have been able to explain those ideas clearly. To make the text accessible, I have avoided using footnotes; but the interested reader will find at the end of the book the sources for the insights and claims on which I rely. The passages discussed in those notes are marked with an asterisk* in the chapter.

In the Grip of a Myth

All round the world, political parties and movements – both on the left and on the right – invoke the will of the people. In 2013 the Abbott government in Australia said that any attempt by the Australian senate to hold up repeal of the carbon tax was opposed to the will of the people; and the One Nation Party claims to be a political party that represents the people of Australia, who are concerned that their will is being ignored by the two-party system. Marine Le Pen of the French National Front asserts that attempts by the French judiciary to examine the party's finances would be opposed to the will of the people. Campaigners for same-sex marriage in Northern Ireland say that opposition to their cause runs against the will of the people. The former President of Venezuela, Hugo Chávez declared in his 2007 inaugural address that the people's judgement is pure, its will is strong, and no one can corrupt or even threaten it. In the wake of the failed military coup in Turkey in 2016, President Erdoğan claimed that the people who come out to demonstrate against the coup were manifesting a singular 'national will'. Speaking of the rise of the US Tea Party, one of its members said that the party had realized that government spending without the will of the people is a form of taxation without representation. Campaigners against the electoral college in the United States say that the college frustrates the will of the people because it can deny victory to the candidate with a majority share of the popular vote, as shown in the election of Donald Trump over Hillary Clinton. The UN ambassador to the United Nations, Nikki Hayley, has said that Trump's recognition of Jerusalem as the capital of Israel 'did the will of the people'.

In the United Kingdom Conservative politicians have enthusiastically discovered the will of the people since the Brexit referendum in 2016. David Davis, the Secretary of State for Exiting the

European Union, repeatedly appeals to the will of the people as a way of warning MPs not to vote against the government's policy. On 15 December 2017, at the conclusion of the European Council meeting, Theresa May tweeted: 'We will deliver on the will of the British people and get the best Brexit deal for our country.' Speaking as foreign secretary, Boris Johnson said, of the opposition to Brexit, that there were those who were determined to stop Brexit and hence to frustrate the will of the people – a mistake, he judged, that would lead to feelings of betrayal. Even those opposed to Brexit have repeatedly asserted that they did not want to disregard the will of the people.

My purpose in writing this book is to convince you – the reader – that the will of the people is a myth. There is no such thing as the will of the people, just as there are no such things as unicorns, flying horses or lost continents called Atlantis. Those who think that accepting the will of the people is an essential part of democratic public life are in the grip of a myth. Worse still, the phrase 'the will of the people' is part of a larger populist myth that assumes that government policy can be decided directly by the people as they exercise their power collectively.

The terms 'populist' and 'populism' are nowadays widely bandied about. They are used to describe very different political movements. The label 'populist' has been applied to UK supporters of Brexit; to European right-wing anti-immigrant parties in countries such as France, Austria and Hungary; to European left-wing anti-austerity parties in Europe, for example Podemos in Spain or Syriza in Greece, or to movements like Occupy Wall Street; to Eurosceptic parties such as Five Star and the Northern League in Italy; to Trump supporters in the United States; or to the left-wing populism of Evo Morales in Bolivia or of the late Hugo Chávez in Venezuela. Given the variety of political ideas and movements in this mix, it often seems as though 'populist' is simply being used as a term of abuse, to describe the politics a speaker disagrees with.

Yet, despite this diversity, the term 'populist'* does pick out, in these otherwise very different movements, certain common elements, invoking a core set of ideas to which different causes are attached. All populists see the prevailing system of representative government as something that has been taken over by an elite. All look to rectify this state of affairs through the direct involvement

4

of ordinary people, whose will should prevail in the making of policy. All think that the will of the people – at least as they claim to understand it – should be the basis of government policy.

For those who are friends of democracy, the claim that the people should be the basis of all political power at first sight seems self-evident. It is a taken-for-granted assumption. Indeed, it seems to define what we mean by democracy. Among these same friends of democracy, there is often a nostalgia for what they imagine was a purer past. They look back to what they suppose were direct democracies – that is, classical Athens in antiquity or, in (pre)modern times, agricultural societies in which an upright people governed itself, as the farmers of early America or the peasants of Europe were once supposed to do. From this perspective the democratic ideal is to replicate in modern, large-scale democracies the earlier practice of government by the assembly of the people so far as is practicable.

So the idea of the will of the people presents itself both as a part of contemporary populist rhetoric and as a nostalgic longing for a lost form of true democracy. If only the people – and not the elites – could be in control of government, all would be well. This is said in bad faith by manipulative political leaders, who are using the appeal to the will of the people to consolidate their own power. It is said in good faith by those friends of democracy who think that the workings of modern-day democracies would be improved through the direct involvement of the mass of citizens. Cynical manipulation married to idealized nostalgia is a dangerous combination. To avoid the cynical manipulation we need to rid ourselves of the idealized nostalgia.

Elitism?

A tactic frequently adopted against anyone who dares question the idea of the will of the people is to accuse the critic of being elitist. To doubt that the will of the people ought to be the basis of government policy is to put yourself above the ordinary person, the man or woman in the street who is entitled to a say in politics.

Since it began to emerge in the first part of the twentieth century, mass democracy has had its elitist critics. Those critics often drew on ideas of the herd psychology of crowds, to which democratic publics were compared. For example, in one of the most widely read books on democracy, a leading writer asserted that, upon entering politics, the typical citizen dropped down to a lower level of mental performance, arguing in a way that he would readily recognize as infantile within the sphere of his real interests.* Even parties on the left, who were supposed to favour the interests of the working class, held that a disciplined vanguard party was needed to prevent false consciousness from slowing down the impending revolution.

Elitist criticisms of democracy have been revived in recent years by political theorists, particularly in the United States, who accuse ordinary citizens in democracies of systematic ignorance.* Basing their findings on public opinion polling, these theorists say that individual voters have no consistent views, are biased and prejudiced, know little about politics and fail to engage with the details of policy. They even try to clinch their case by saying that the trouble with these voters is that they do not understand the principles of orthodox economics! (Presumably, the thought is that such knowledge would reconcile the poor to their economic lot.) The same critics go on

7

to argue that voters should be required to take an examination to acquire the right to vote, or that the more qualified should be given more votes than the less qualified. In all this, they seem happy to ignore the well-known abuse of voter registration requirements – which were used over decades to deprive African American voters of their right to vote – as well as the increasingly malign influence of money in US politics, both on the left and on the right – an influence through which the effectiveness of the political liberties of the citizen is undermined.

So, to be absolutely clear, nothing in this book requires you to believe in such jaundiced views of the people. Of course, in every society you can find those who are ignorant and loud-mouth. Saloon bar cynicism too often passes for political intelligence. But such people are found on all sides of political debate. To admit this is nowhere near saying that voters in general are ignorant or short-sighted. In my experience, the vast majority of people are prudent, responsible and self-sufficient. They do their jobs diligently, often with good humour, even when those jobs are boring or underpaid. They spend within their means. They bring up their children with love and concern, if (naturally) with some overindulgence. When the need arises, they willingly help relatives and neighbours. They care for their pets and rescue wounded wild animals. They keep their property in good order. They want the best for their country, their fellow citizens and the next generation. They also pay taxes. No taxation without representation is a good principle. The will of the people is a myth not because the general run of people in a democracy are ignorant and short-sighted, but because people are diverse and there are different and often incompatible ways of combining their opinions. 'The people' is made up of a plurality of people, and there is no simple way of getting from the plural to the singular.

Citizens Voice Their Discontent

Populists are right to worry about elites and their control of the economy and politics. Between 1980 and 2016*, in the United States, Canada and Western Europe, the top 1 per cent of income earners captured 28 per cent of the increase in overall income in that period, whereas the bottom 50 per cent captured only 9 per cent of the increase. In the United States the figures are more striking. There the top 1 per cent captured as much as the bottom 88 per cent. In short, over the last thirty-five years, an economic elite has found ways of capturing a larger share of the growth of national incomes.

But statistics tell only part of the story. As important as the increase in economic inequality is the social dislocation that comes with the decline of manufacturing in societies such as France, Italy, the United States and the United Kingdom. During the French presidential election campaign of 2017, Emmanuel Macron went to meet union representatives from the Whirlpool factory in Amiens, which employed nearly three hundred people but was threatened with closure. At the same time Marine Le Pen, his National Front rival for the presidency, appeared on a picket line outside the factory itself, urging that Macron had shown contempt to the pickets by not visiting them himself. Macron did later visit the factory, but the incident with Le Pen was one small example of the ability of populists to tap into the discontent created by economic change and the decline of manufacturing. In towns and cities where people make things, there is more to life than the income the job brings in. There is the pride that goes with knowing that you are working in order to provide for your family. There is the friendship and comradeliness that come from working with others. The place where you work gives you a sense of local identity. You are the town where porcelain is made, where steel is fired or where fabrics are spun. When the local factory goes, there is a large hole left that is seldom filled quickly. The jobs lost may not be recovered for a generation or more.

Immigration, too, can threaten one's sense of place. There is too easy an assumption, on the liberal left of politics, that to be concerned about immigration is to be racist. This is to deny what, for some citizens, is the lived perplexity of their experience. If you live in the town where you grew up and you start to see shops opening in streets that you have known since childhood, conducting their business in a foreign language and trading in goods that are strange to you, you literally – literally – do not understand what is happening around you. If your perplexity is compounded by pressure on schools and hospitals and other public services, then you may well think that, in order to solve your problems, all the government needs to do is to control immigration. A fast pace of change associated with a decline in public services turns incomprehension into resentment.

For many people in such communities, political representation over many years was secured by parties of the centre-left. However, the reputation of those parties with their traditional supporters was damaged during their terms of office in the United Kingdom, the United States and France in the wake of the 2008 global financial crisis and 2010 Euro crisis. Balancing the government books inhibited the public spending that might have boosted the economy, were it not for the fear that too much borrowing should damage the credit ratings of governments. Policy responsibility then fell on the central banks. They used the only tools they had available: cheap money through the purchase of bonds. The effect was to send the investment houses looking for higher returns in equities and property, boosting the holdings of those who already held these assets. Workers in many places found themselves squeezed, often with their jobs moving to countries where labour was cheap. Austerity in government spending worsened the public services on which they relied. In some countries rising house prices driven by low interest rates and speculative investment made it hard for many to buy a house. New political movements on the left sought to persuade people that austerity was the key issue; those on the right, that it was immigration. The puzzle is not why so many started to look to new movements outside the centre-left for political representation; the puzzle is why they did not look sooner.

In Hungary the populist Viktor Orbán* refused to debate policy before the elections of 2010 and 2014, saying that no policy-specific debates were needed because the alternatives facing the country were so obvious. What was needed instead was 'thirty robust lads who start working to implement what we all know needs to be done'. In the United States Donald Trump promised to drain the swamp and make America great again. In the United Kingdom Brexiteers promise to 'take back control' of immigration and trade policy, so that all would be well. But the policy problems thrown up by changing global production patterns in mature economies are not as easy to solve as populist promises are easy to make.

The populism on which general appeals to the will of the people rest is an unrealistic response to the dilemmas that many citizens experience. The people cannot control government policy in any meaningful sense and all governments have to deal with the world as it is, not with the world as many would want it to be. The social and economic ills at the root of populism are serious, but that does not mean that we need the idea of the will of the people, acting like a thread to string together the key tenets of populism. It is a mythical thread, the fascination with which distracts us from the reforms to our political system that would make that system work for the common good. We need to be disabused of the myth.

2

Nostalgic Myths

In the Presence of the People

Shortly after he became president of France, Emmanuel Macron visited Greece, where he addressed an audience in Athens. In an assured performance he surprised everyone by beginning his speech in Greek, before switching to French. Against the night sky, the Parthenon behind him and a young crowd in front of him, the place from which Macron spoke was well chosen. It was the Pnyx. The Pnyx is the hill on which the assembly (*ekklēsia*) of citizens in ancient Athens met to debate and decide on their common affairs. The symbolism was obvious. After the years in which Greece's modern-day democracy had been subject to the harsh disciplines of the European monetary order, Macron's presidency represented a new beginning for Europe, a new beginning that was to be built on the principles of democracy. Modern ambition was dignified by the image of an ancient source. Political renewal was underpinned by a reminder of democratic origins, in particular by an image of democracy in which the people governed themselves directly. Democracy was to be conducted in the presence of the people.

Populism lives by the thought that the presence of the people in government is sufficient to wrest control from an unrepresentative elite. The movement of protest against the banks and finance industry, Occupy Wall Street, is the clearest example of this politics of presence in physical form, with scores of Occupy movements springing up after the first occupation of Wall Street and of the nearby Zuccotti Park. The assumption is that, when the people take back control of the streets, the forces of elite control will be defeated.

But a politics of popular presence can also take virtual form through social media, where seemingly personal encounters mimic real encounters.

Why does Donald Trump tweet so much? Why do his supporters love it when he does? It is because a tweet gives the illusion of a direct relationship between leader and follower. For the follower, the tweet is addressed just to him- or herself, with no intermediary. The follower imagines a personal relationship with the president. The pretence of presence and the personalization of power go hand in hand.

Macron himself is interesting in this respect. He is commonly regarded as the politician who first started to turn the tide of populism in Europe in 2017 with his defeat of Marine Le Pen in the French presidential election. Yet Macron's own route to victory borrowed much from the populist manual. He created a new party from scratch, drawing in people who had not been involved in party politics previously but had been active in civil society groups. The new party was to represent the people between and beyond the established parties. Its original name, En Marche, conjured up the image of a movement going forward. And, of course, the contest for the French presidency personalizes an election better than anything else. When he stood on the Pnyx, he seemed to be the reincarnation of democratic orators in ancient fifth-century BCE Athens, who sought to persuade the citizens to make their political choices when assembled together. In doing so, he relied on Greek myths.

Greek Myths

Between 508 and 338 BCE, though with several interruptions, ancient Athens practised government by the assembly of eligible citizens. Political decisions were made by those citizens gathered together in one place to discuss and take a vote on what should be done. The key institution, the assembly, consisted of the entire population of male Athenian citizens, hence all of them were entitled to attend its meetings. At the beginning of the fifth century, the assembly met ten times a year; by its end, the meetings were sometimes as many as forty. The political constitution of Athens divided the city-state into ten 'tribes'; and each tribe was responsible for presiding over the assembly, in rotation. The agenda for debate in the meetings was drawn up by an executive body, the Council (*boulē*), but it could be amended. The scope of the assembly's power was wide; it included war and peace, the currency, and customs duties. Once all those who wanted to speak had spoken, a vote was taken by a show of hands. The assembly also elected important public officials, most notably the generals, although many public offices were filled through a lottery system. In a democracy, it was said, citizens took turns at governing and being governed.

Many see the Athenian government by assembly as the original and most influential image of direct democracy.* One reason for this view is that, while ancient Athenians were economically astute and intellectually vibrant, they were also great self-publicists. Here is an example of that self-publicity – a piece of it that the great historian Thucydides put into the mouth of the political leader Pericles.* At the end of the first year of fighting a war against the Athenians' great rival, Sparta, Pericles is reported as saying:

> Here each individual is interested not only in his own affairs but in the affairs of state as well: even those who are mostly occupied with their own business are extremely well-informed on general politics – this is a peculiarity of ours: we do not say that a man who

takes no interest in politics is a man who minds his own business; we say that he has no business here at all. (Thucydides 2.43.3)

Praise for direct democracy in ancient Athens has elevated this Periclean assertion down the centuries, making it echo and resound among some of the greatest political thinkers who have ever written.

Virtually everyone these days accepts that assembly government of the sort practised in ancient Athens cannot be replicated in large-scale contemporary societies. Yet people still think that its model of direct democracy sets an ideal to follow today. If only we could find some way of assembling the people – or a sample of them – to get them to make political decisions, we would overcome the weaknesses of representative government.

There is a simple problem with this argument, however. It is not just that direct democracy cannot be practised in the modern world; it was not practised in ancient Athens either. It is well known that ancient Athens excluded women from any participation in politics; they certainly had no right of participating in the assembly.

Excluded from citizenship, of course, were slaves, as were the so called 'metics', the resident foreign workers; and Pericles' law of 451 BCE excluded from citizenship all those whose mother and father were not, both, full citizens (a criterion that eliminated many Athenians born to aristocratic foreign mothers – such as the famous Agariste in Pericles' own ancestry). Those who write about Athenian democracy usually note these facts, and then pass on to the practice of Athenian government, as though these exclusions were a matter of detail. So it is a sober exercise to look at the actual numbers, which can be found in Table 2.1. The estimates are for the years around 430 BCE.

Comparing the number of citizens to that of the total population, *only between one in seven and one in five* of the total were citizens. In our days a ratio like that would obviously disqualify a society as a democracy. But this is not the end of the problem. Even if we take the lower estimate of 30,000 citizens, only a fraction of them could have participated in the assembly at any one time. The Pnyx was large enough to contain only 6,000 people at a time. Government by the assembly of all citizens was literally impossible.

THE WILL OF THE PEOPLE

Table 2.1. Population and Citizenship in Ancient Athens

Category	Numbers[a]
Total population	215,000–300,000
Slaves	80,000–110,000
Metics and families	25,000–40,000
Citizens and their families	80,000–110,000
Adult male citizens	30,000–45,000

SOURCE: Victor Ehrenberg, *The Greek State*, 2nd edn (London: Methuen, 1969), p. 31.

[a] The figures are estimates of ranges, so they cannot simply be added together.

Why does this matter? The Athenian democracy is not all that it has been cracked up to be; so what? After all, it was a substantial achievement at the time, and we can still find inspiration in its ideals even if their implementation was flawed. But an ideal that no one can come close to realizing ceases to be an ideal and becomes a falsehood sustaining an impossible vision. In this case, the falsehood implies that there is something second best about representative democracy – which happens only because representative democracy is being judged against an idealized myth.

Rousseau's Will

There is a story told of the great nineteenth-century philosopher and historian Thomas Carlyle. Sitting one evening at a dinner when everyone was discussing in a typically English way the irrelevance of theory to practice, Carlyle silenced the conversation with a few words: 'There was once a man called Rousseau. He printed a book of political theories, and the nobles of that land laughed. But the second edition was bound in their skins.' The book was *The Social Contract*, originally published in 1762. If you were going to choose anyone to be the great theorist of the will of the people, that would have been Rousseau. Scholars still discuss today what his influence on the French Revolution precisely was for Carlyle to refer to it in this manner. Yet there is no doubt that, out of all political thinkers, Rousseau crafted the most influential account of the will of the people. Virtually all later writing on the subject is a set of variations on his themes.

Rousseau distinguished between what he called the 'will of all' and the 'general will'. The will of all expresses the opinions of citizens when they are looking at political matters from their own point of view. There can be as many wills forming the will of all as there are individuals. The general will, by contrast, is formed when citizens are trying to decide what is in their common interest. The idea can be illustrated by an example that Rousseau himself uses.

Imagine a group of citizens in a political association having to decide whether to have capital punishment or not. According to Rousseau, in order to find the general will, each person will reason as follows. Either we should have capital punishment or we should not. If we have capital punishment, then I am less likely to be a victim of the crime of murder. (Rousseau assumes that capital punishment acts as a deterrent.) On the other hand, if we have capital punishment, I will be liable to the death penalty in the event that I commit a murder. (Rousseau was nothing if not impartial in his view of human nature.) So finding the general will requires me to balance these two points of view. I think of the benefits and the costs of having the practice of capital punishment against the benefits and the costs of not having it. That is how I and others can find the general will.

Rousseau himself thought that, when people went through this chain of reasoning about capital punishment, they would agree that the state had the right to take life in the case of murder. His view on that particular question, however, is less important than his approach to finding the general will. What he recommends as a way of deciding public issues makes a lot of sense in democratic terms. When we vote in an election or in a referendum, we should not be thinking about our own interests but about the common good. In fact, as his example of capital punishment shows, often thinking about the common good turns out to be a way of thinking about our own good, given all the changes we go through in life. We may grumble about paying our taxes, but we are pleased that the hospital is there and well staffed when we fall ill, the school well provided for when our children need education, and our pensions safe at the end of our working life. Rousseau's general will is enlightened self-interest by another name.

If Rousseau was so right, why can we not follow him all the way? Why not say that the general will is the will of the people and that, if the general will is geared to the common good, the will of the people should form the basis of government policy? What is so mythical about that line of argument?

The short answer is that Rousseau was far too optimistic about a consensus emerging from citizens who sought the general will. Towards the end of *The Social Contract*, he wrote that, when new laws are being considered in a well-ordered community, '[t]he first man to propose them merely says what all have already felt' (book 4, ch. 1).* A consensus will emerge in societies where people regard themselves as a single body; and Rousseau writes lyrically about bands of peasants regulating their affairs under the oak tree and always acting wisely. On those occasions when there is no immediate consensus, individuals in a minority, who are really thinking about the general will, should realize that, because they are in a minority, they have simply mistaken the general will. (We will come back to this argument in Chapter 6.)

Even in the sort of societies that Rousseau had in mind, ones with people sharing an agricultural way of life, his expectation of spontaneous consensus was always romantic. There is a fine study of a small and isolated Swiss agricultural community called Törbel,* exactly the sort of community that Rousseau had in mind. Yet the author of that study highlights the deep differences, pervasive and long-standing, that can exist in such a community. Inhabitants of Törbel would remember with bitterness how the grandparents of different families took different sides in the Swiss Civil War. Despite their differences, people could still negotiate with one another about their common affairs, since life is hard in such communities and there have to be common rules. Grazing rights have to be settled and steep terraces have to be maintained, otherwise all will suffer. But it was harsh necessity that created consensus, not the spontaneous meeting of wills. Even when people share a common life, they do not share a common point of view.

Democratic Myths

Both classical Athens and small-scale agricultural societies have provided powerful images of what democracy might be like. The problem is that

27

these images are a barrier to coherent thinking about modern democracy. From the example of Athens, people take the idea that the assembled body of citizens should decide on what the government is to do and that anything short of that ideal is second best. From Rousseau's thinking, people take the idea that the sovereignty of the people is exercised through their general will. Both ideas are myths. Of the adult males who constituted Athens' citizen body, only a minority would have been able to meet in assembly and discuss their common affairs. Within the agricultural communities that Rousseau thought were communities of virtue, there can be deep divisions and differences. Yet, when these mythical images take a grip on one's thoughts, one is often driven to a view of democracy in which the will of the people will triumph through that people's direct involvement in decision-making.

To escape the myths, we need to answer three questions. What is a people? Can there be such a thing as the will of a people? And, even if there is a will of the people, what follows from this for the democratic duties of citizens? Realistic answers to these questions lead to anti-populist conclusions, as we shall see in the next four chapters. In the end it is not myths we need, but clear-headed thinking about our present circumstances and conditions.

3

What Is a People?

Singular of Plural?

If you are going to talk about the will of the people, you need to understand what you mean when you refer to 'the people'. However, being clear about the meaning of 'the people' is hard because 'people' is one of those tricky words that get used in two quite different ways. Sometimes, when we talk about people, we are thinking of separate individual human beings. For example, we might say that some people put sugar in their tea and other people do not. If we like, we can count the people in a room who fall into each category; but, despite the categories, we are thinking about these people as separate individuals.

At other times the word clearly designates 'the people' as a single body that acts as one. Anyone who has ever watched an American courtroom drama will know that the criminal case is brought in the name of the people, as in the 2015 film *The People vs Fritz Bauer*. The sense of 'the people' used here is a collective one. It is not the case that individual US citizens are bringing the action; the action is being brought by the public authorities in the name of the corporate group known as 'the people'.

A useful way of telling whether someone is talking about 'people' as different individuals who share a common characteristic or about 'the people' as a group regarded as a corporate body is to consider whether it makes sense to ask 'how many people' are involved. For example, the number of English people who put sugar in their tea has dropped in recent years. We can do these counts because we know that, when we talk about English people, we are really talking about different people who happen to be English. By contrast, it makes no sense to ask: 'How many US citizens are involved in the court action against Fritz Bauer?'. The public authorities are acting in the name of the whole, not in the name of a collection of parts. This was clear in the original German title of the film, which is *Der Staat gegen Fritz Bauer* (*The State vs Fritz Bauer*).

In social and political life, it is often convenient to think of different people who form a single group as making a common decision. For example, if the members of a sports club at their annual general meeting decide to raise the club's subscription, we can say that 'the membership' has decided to raise the subscription. We can say this even if many members were not present and there was a flaming row among those who were. If we say that the membership has decided, what we are really saying is that those who were entitled to participate in the decision went through and accepted a decision process that resulted in a collective choice to raise the subscription. But it is generally a bit of a mouthful to spell out the meaning of corporate terms like 'the membership' or 'the people', and so we stick with the convention of talking of different people making a decision together as though they were one person. We replace the plural by the singular.

In social and political life, it is very convenient to think of the people living in a country as forming one body, as the example of US criminal prosecutions goes to show. Many useful activities require a high degree of coordination and acceptance of conventional ways of doing things among the members of society. Members of parliament promise to serve their constituents even when they do not know personally the vast majority of those constituents. Countries enter into international agreements with one another on the understanding that the government signing the treaty is signing for the whole country, acting in the name of the citizens taken collectively. The reason for adopting these conventions is simple. If individuals can be committed to a common course of action under some authority, they can achieve, collectively, far more than they could achieve individually. Indeed, there are some important goals that can only be achieved collectively. It takes whole states to make agreements among themselves on behalf of those whom they represent – agreements such as to reduce greenhouse gas emissions and to hold out any hope of slowing down global climate change.

However, no matter how useful the shorthand of saying that, when the public authorities are acting on our behalf, they are acting for the whole body of citizens, we also need to remember that political action often involves the semblance of people acting as one when in fact the individuals who make up the corporate body are divided. When people wished to protest against the UK government's involvement in the war in Iraq, they marched under the slogan 'Not in My Name'. Yet, in one sense, the war was in their name. The UK government had committed the body of UK citizens to the war by virtue of its political authority. In another sense, however, the war was not in the name of those who opposed it. In the corporate sense, 'the British people' was committed; yet not all British people were committed. We can make this distinction, because we recognize a difference between the people regarded as members of a common body and the individual people who made up that common body. We can recognize that behind the singular is the plural.

Populists add a twist to the distinction between people as individuals and the people as a single body. They contrast 'the people' with the elite, be it an economic or a political elite. For populists the vast mass of the population that lives in a country forms a common body, whose interests are being ignored by a minority that actually run the country: the bankers, the big companies, the

34

out-of-touch and corrupt politicians, and so on. Often particular groups among the people are made to stand for the whole: Main Street versus Wall Street, Britain's hard-working families, the small man, and so on. Behind the inhabitants of the country stands the heartland* of the people, who are the authentic bearers of the title. There is a superficial plurality, but the reference is singular.

Nationalist ways of thinking build on this substitution of 'people', plural, with 'the people', singular. In nationalist ways of thinking, the world is populated by groups who may be regarded as separate peoples. Differences exist between peoples, but each people forms a distinct group. Differences within a country are downplayed by comparison to differences between countries.

The problem with this downplaying of differences within a country is that a country only functions successfully as a political unit when the main bulk of its population – the individuals who make up the body of citizens – identifies with its system of government. Where that basic sense of identification is lacking, the government does not function. During the First World War, the whole of Ireland was in the United Kingdom.

The British government did not introduce conscription into Ireland in 1916, as it did in the rest of the United Kingdom, because it knew that a large number of Irish citizens would simply have refused to serve. Ireland was part of the United Kingdom as a result of historical processes of colonization and integration that had been going on for centuries. For most of the British Isles, those same processes had resulted in politically successful integration. It was the complex combination of nationalism and Catholicism in Ireland that made the situation there different. Similar processes of integration and incorporation are true of virtually every state in the world. If we talk about 'the French people' or 'the people of China', we are referring to groups of people who now form one body as the result of military conquest, peaceful political union, or some combination of both, sometimes going back over many centuries. State action constructs a people.

One Out of Many?

In 1854, a guide to the Mézenc region* of France, some 350 miles south of Paris, recommended viewing the area from a balloon, but 'only if the aeronaut can remain out of range of a rifle' – or else he or she would be attacked by the locals. Nowadays the Auvergne tourist organization invites visitors to discover the pure source of the Loire. In the middle of the nineteenth century fewer than half of all French schoolchildren spoke French. Instead they would speak local dialects and languages like Breton, Alsatian, Occitan or French Flemish. In response, the French government made French the official language of instruction in schools and made instruction in civics obligatory. This was a process of turning peasants into Frenchmen.* Those whom we know to form 'the people of France' are the product of state authority and cultural instruction. The French national anthem refers to *enfants de la patrie*, the children of the country. The citizens are only children of the country because, as children, they were educated by the French republic.

The story of France is replicated by other nations. The countries who make up the United Nations are 'nations' because they have been created through political action. Given a different history, the nations of the world would not be the same as they currently are: they would not have the same boundaries or be inhabited by the same types of people. (Iceland is a probable exception to this generalization, but there are not many such exceptions.) The creation of today's nations sometimes involves fusion, as in the case of Germany and Italy in the nineteenth century, and sometimes fission, as in the case of Great Britain and Ireland in 1922. Peoples alter their identity at different periods, as inhabitants are willing to come together and form one new people or to separate and form two new peoples. In recent years, among many of the peoples previously absorbed into larger political units, breakaway movements have grown, favouring separation and independence – for example among Catalans in Spain, Flemish in Belgium, or Scots in the United Kingdom. The separation of the world into peoples is not a natural fact but the result of government policy, political movements and social change.

Of course the fact that the country in which you were raised is the product of a particular political history need not reduce your identification with that country and its citizens. Early impressions shape the mind and the sentiments. Growing up in a place helps to turn different individuals into parts of a people. For example, like many other Brits, I felt pleasure and pride at the opening of the London Olympics in 2012 even though I personally avoid James Bond films, have some reservations about the institution of the monarchy and do not believe the NHS to be the envy of the world. Many people in other countries enjoyed the show; only Brits, like me, could rejoice that *we* had done something right.

Identification with a country does not mean unanimity in political opinion, however. The political culture of a country is defined by the conflicts and contradictions it contains. Britain does not have the Catholic–republican conflicts of France or the Protestant–Catholic conflicts of Germany. For most of the past hundred years, British conflicts have been class-based, with some residue of the nineteenth-century conflict between non-conformity and the Church of England and, more recently, differences of nationality associated with devolution and secession. Identifying with your country does not mean that you agree with everyone else. It means that you understand your country's political disputes and you normally know which side in those disputes you are inclined to take.

Creating a nation and the corresponding sense of peoplehood among the inhabitants of a country normally involves two processes. One process consists of extending and strengthening the rights of citizenship for those who belong to the country. Members of the same political community are given equal civil rights as citizens, so that there is the same rule of law for all, whether they be nobility or commoners, clergy or laypeople. That is how the modern European state distinguished itself from the feudal systems of the Middle Ages. Then come political rights, most obviously the right to vote, complemented by social rights such as financial security in old age or medical care in the case of ill health. The sequencing of the creation of these rights varies. Bismarck's Germany provided social insurance for health and old age in the 1880s before the arrival of democracy, whereas the United Kingdom's welfare state had to wait until the 1940s, after the establishment of democracy, for its full development. Significantly, two key policies of the welfare state were called *national* insurance and a *national* health service.

The second process consists of defining national identities by exclusion. In the crucial period between 1890 and 1930, when immigration was high, there was a process of making Americans.* Immigration policy was built on the assumption that certain 'races' were unfit to migrate to the United States. Chinese and Japanese immigrants were denied rights of citizenship; and quotas were placed on migrants from different European countries, favouring northern Protestant countries over southern and Catholic ones. These exclusions were not an incidental feature of the nation-building process; they were integral to it. When Trump tries to ban Muslims entering the United States, he is not defying American tradition, he is re-enacting it.

Against this background of inclusion through social rights and exclusion through migration policy, it is not surprising that populist parties often mobilize around questions of economic security and immigration. The rights of citizenship, particularly the social rights of citizenship, protect existing citizens from the cold winds of economic competition. Migration policies define who gets to enjoy those rights. Hostility to immigrant labour brings these two themes together. Commentators are sometimes surprised that populist parties take a left-wing stance on social and economic policy, protecting pensions and employment rights, but right-wing positions on immigration and cultural policy. The French National Front is one example, as is Austria's Freedom Party or Australia's One Nation Party. But commentators should not be surprised. Populists have to tell a story of peoplehood in order to promote their cause. Usually they identify some particular groups as the heart of the people, distinguishing them from other inhabitants. For example, they identify the people as Christian but not as Muslims, or the Australian people as white but not as Asian or aboriginal. Economic security for the heartland, with its clear boundaries that distinguish that heartland from aliens within and without, tells a powerful political story.

Combining Peoples

Because the creation of nation-states is a complex historical process, the idea that there is a single will of the people breaks down. This is not so much a matter of different individuals taking different views. If individuals in a state feel themselves to be at one with others in that state, then voting and political bargaining are obvious ways of dealing with disagreement (though we shall see in the next chapter that even in such conditions life is not so simple). What happens, however, when one state comprises individuals who identify with different peoples or nations? Is the will of the people to be equated with the decision of the adult citizens who are members of the state, or should it be equated with the separate wills of separate peoples?

Until recently the United Kingdom has been a unitary state, but one with a special status for Northern Ireland after partition in 1922. In its early years, Northern Ireland had a different system of election for its government; the chief executive of the government was known as 'prime minister' and many public services were run on different lines from those of the United Kingdom as a whole. Its political parties were organized on completely different principles from those of the rest of the United Kingdom, reflecting the continuing existence of the national issue. During the 'troubles' of the 1970s and 1980s, the UK government, which by then had taken back political responsibility from

the Stormont government, introduced intern-
ment without trial, a measure that would have
been unthinkable in Great Britain. To be sure,
Northern Ireland has always had the same laws
on social security and taxation as the rest of the
United Kingdom, but its distinctive identity is
marked in many ways.

Since 1997 devolution has reinforced the separate identities of the constituent units of the
United Kingdom. Three or four decades ago,
people would refer to the 'British people' without
any sense of impropriety, intending to include
all those who now form the nations – plural –
of the United Kingdom. So, even if individuals
can be said to be members of a separate people,
it does not follow that the government of the
United Kingdom should take its decisions simply
by reference to the balance of opinion among
individual citizens. Since the composite nations
of the United Kingdom have been given separate
status as nations in their own right as regards
devolved matters, we no longer have public policy
based on the will of the British people all across
the board. We have policies for the peoples of the
United Kingdom. You cannot rely on the will
of the people to resolve questions until you have

defined the relevant peoples. And, even if you can define the relevant peoples, determining the right balance of opinion is complex, as we shall see in the next chapter.

4

Majority Willing?

Why Politics?

We need politics to ensure that we have those good things of life that we can only have in common. External defence and internal law and order require a common authority. Education and healthcare, transport and flood protection need to be organized for all. Some say that markets can supply many of these things as well as, or even better than, the state. But markets need laws to govern them, rules of property to define who owns what, and ways of remedying and preventing problems with faulty goods, misleading advertising, or commercial fraud. Of necessity, living in a society means that governments make common decisions for all.

If everyone agreed on these common decisions, there would be no problem. As we have seen in chapter 2, this is what Rousseau imagined happening in peasant societies governed by the general will when laws are proposed: '[t]he first man to propose them merely says what all have already felt'. It was a romantic thought when Rousseau wrote it; it is a hopelessly utopian thought these days. People have conflicting opinions and interests, and these need to be reconciled by some method if common policies are to be adopted. People cannot just go their own separate ways. Yet, when people have different opinions, they risk deadlock, unless they can agree to a common course of action in the face of disagreement. They need a way to make a common decision on policy, accepting that there are different and incompatible views about what should be done.

Majority Rule

One obvious way to resolve policy disagreements is to take a vote and to go with the opinion of the majority. If a sports club has enough money to refurbish the bar or to repaint the outside of the building, but not to do both, then why not let the members decide by majority vote? When parliaments pass laws, they usually do so by a majority of MPs' votes. If there is a region of a country in which there is strong pressure for independence, then why not hold a referendum, as has happened twice in Québec over its status in Canada, and accept what the majority decides? To answer this question, we need to look at the principle of majority rule.

Majority rule says that a group should decide some common course of action according to the choice of 50 per cent plus one of those voting. If 49 club members out of 100 decide that it is better to refurbish the bar than repaint the outside and 51 members decide that painting the outside of the building is better than refurbishing the bar, then the painting is what should be done.

Majority rule has two attractive qualities. Because it relies solely on the number of voters and not on which particular individuals are voting, it treats each voter the same way. If a minority of long-standing club members is given a veto over spending decisions, then the decision would be biased towards their preferences. For example, they might be more likely to favour refurbishing the bar than painting the outside. By contrast, with majority rule, everyone counts as one and no one counts as more than one. This rule gives each and every individual equal standing in the making of the club's decisions.

Majority rule also treats all alternatives in the same way, including the status quo. If a majority of voters wishes to move away from the status quo, then the body that makes the decision will change its policy. Any rule that requires a higher threshold for change than a simple majority rule is known as a 'supermajority' rule. For example, if 60 per cent of voters are required to agree before there is change, then there is an obvious bias in favour of the status quo. Those who are comfortable with things as they are have an advantage over those who are not.

So majority rule gives equal standing to individuals when they are making a common decision and prevents the status quo from having a privileged position. For these reasons it captures a basic sense of political equality. Neither some voters nor the alternatives that some voters favour are privileged. The ideal of political equality is a central principle of democracy. In consequence, majority rule seems to be required by democracy.

Democracy implies political equality and political equality implies majority rule, since majority rule is impartial with respect to individuals and alternatives. Moreover, it is the *only* rule that has these qualities.* In short, if you are a committed democrat, you believe in political equality in voting. If you believe in political equality in voting, it seems that you are committed to majority rule.

Does this mean that majority rule gives us the will of the people? Can we equate the will of the people with what the majority prefers? The answer is 'no'. Apart from the very simple cases in which a group of people have to choose between two and only two given alternatives, we may not be able to determine what it is that a majority prefers. And if we cannot determine what a majority prefers, we cannot equate the will of the people with the choice of the majority. To explain how this is so, I shall tell you the parable of a fictional country called Folkland.

The Parable of Folkland

Once upon a time, political life in Folkland was simple. Like many other comparatively well-off

Table 4.1. Political Preferences in Folkland

Left	Right	Total
55%	45%	100%

countries in the second half of the twentieth century, Folkland had developed a welfare state, which provided education, social security and healthcare for all. This welfare state was popular. When asked, 55 per cent of voters generally inclined towards an expansion of the welfare state that involved the raising of taxes, while 45 per cent favoured a reduction in taxes with some trimming back of the welfare state. Those who favoured welfare state expansion tended to support the party of the left; those who were more cautious tended to support the party of the right. These preferences are shown in Table 4.1.

However, voter preferences were not entirely rigid. Both the left-wing party and the right-wing party recognized the popularity of the welfare state and its influence on the way people cast their votes. As a result, they competed with each other, largely on the promise of managing the welfare state better than the rival party. The left-wing party favoured expanding the state as quickly as possible, whereas the right-wing party was inclined to reduce its activities where possible. However, many right-wing voters were sympathetic to the basic principle of a welfare state, even though they grumbled when they paid their taxes; and at the same time a large bulk of voters on the left did not want taxes to rise too far too fast. In consequence, both parties recognized that they could not stray too far from those voters whose inclination was centrist. 'In this tranquil system, boring politics is the price that contented voters pay for reasonably satisfying results.'*

Then politics started to change in Folkland. New young voters joined the electorate. World events also played their part. A major war that involved an ally and in which Folkland participated provoked antiwar reaction among some sections of the population. New issues emerged. Many people favoured protecting nature more. Women wanted equality to extend more widely, many questioning traditional forms of marriage and the segregation between men and women in matters of work. Technology began to undermine the job security of the working classes. The protection of civil liberties became important to well-educated sections of the population. A significant minority wanted the legalization of recreational drug use.

As a result of these changes, political alignments among citizens began to change. On both the left and the right, some responded positively to the new issues, while others continued to favour traditional morality, protection of jobs over protection of the environment and policies that enforced strong law and order. Among those who had previously regarded themselves as being on the left, a significant number took up the new positive responses and called themselves the New Left. Those on the right were generally more resistant to these changes; nevertheless, some of them saw an opportunity to create a political movement that stressed low taxes and low welfare but adopted liberal policies on gender and drug use. They formed the New Right.

So now there were four broad political groupings. The left had split into an Old Left, which remained socially conservative but in favour of the welfare state, and a New Left, which embraced a liberal social morality. The right had split into two groups as well – an Old Right, which remained socially conservative and fiscally prudent, and a

Table 4.2. From Two-Party Politics to Four-Party Politics

	Left	Right	Totals
Old	35%	40%	75%
New	20%	5%	25%
Totals	55%	45%	100%

New Right, which added liberal social morality to its fiscal hawkishness. Voters broke down into four groups that replaced the previous two; the patterns of their opinions is shown in Table 4.2. Two new parties emerged to represent these different strands of opinion. There was now a party of the New Left as well as that of the Old Left, and a party of the New Right as well as that of the Old Right. The Old Left Party now averaged 35 per cent of the vote, the Old Right Party 40 per cent, the New Left Party 20 per cent and the New Right Party 5 per cent.

Since the people of Folkland were democrats, they thought that policy should be made according to the will of the majority, which some were inclined to call the will of the people. The trouble was that, confronted with a pattern of opinion like that in Table 4.2, they disagreed as to what the will of the majority meant. Some thought that the government ought to be formed by the party with the single largest number of votes. The majority vote was identified with the plurality vote, the vote of the single largest group of electors. Those who favoured this plurality principle pointed out that some electoral systems, like the one used in the United Kingdom, regularly gave a majority of seats in parliament to parties with a share of around 40 per cent of the vote, and even less on some occasions. Why not accept that the will of the people is given by the policy positions of the largest single group of voters? On this view, majority rule is equal to the plurality principle, which then defines the will of the people.

By contrast, others pointed out that an absolute majority would require at least two of the political groups to join in some sort of governing coalition. Only governing coalitions representing a majority of the electorate could really claim to conform to the principle of majority rule.

However, yet others pointed out that, while the Old Right Party might have a strong majority for the socially conservative part of its programme, it did not have a majority for the part of its programme that meant cutting the welfare state. Both Old Left and New Left voters, comprising 55 per cent of the total, would oppose that policy. In consequence, this third group argued for a government programme based on a version of the majority principle in which each type of issue was voted on separately. That would lead to an issue-by-issue majority, made up of the overlapping votes of those who were socially conservative but favoured welfare state expansion. By this argument the majority position was that of the Old Left, which offered a programme coextensive with that of the issue-by-issue majority.

The debate was not about whether majority rule was the right principle. All the participants thought of themselves as majoritarians. The debate was about what was meant by majority rule. Supporters of the plurality rule pointed out that a government programme based on that rule would always have the support of the single largest block of voters and, if majority rule meant anything, it meant rule by the greater number. Supporters of the absolute majority rule argued that only a joint programme between parties supported by more than half the voters would be consistent with majority rule. Supporters of the issue-by-issue majority rule argued that, if either of the other rules were adopted, then the majority of voters on each issue would be prevented from getting their way.

Going in Circles

While debate raged in Folkland about the meaning of majority rule when no political grouping had an overall majority, the parties in parliament were trying to form a government. Those parties had seats in exact proportion to the votes they had gained in the most recent election. No party wanted to form a minority government, so a coalition was needed. Since no party could guarantee a government programme that represented its first preference, any coalition that was going to form would depend on the second, third and fourth preferences of the parties. For example, suppose the Old Left Party had to decide which coalitions it might enter. The decision it took on that question depended on whether it cared more for its tax-welfare position, in which case it would

Table 4.3. Preferences for Forming Coalitions

Old Left	•Old Right; New Left; New Right
New Left	•New Right; Old Left; Old Right
Old Right	•New Right; Old Left; New Left
New Right	•New Left; Old Right; Old Left

prefer to join the New Left Party, or for its position on social morality, in which case it would prefer to form a coalition with the Old Right Party. Similar considerations applied to the other parties. For example, the Old Right Party had to decide on whether its tax stance was more important than its stance on social morality. Each party had a preference for the policy platforms of the other parties, depending on which elements were more or less attractive and moving from most favourable to least favourable. The pattern is set out in Table 4.3.

Notice that we can easily understand these preferences. Each party is least likely to go into coalition with the party that is diametrically opposed to it on both dimensions of policy difference. The two 'new' parties care more about getting their way on social morality than they do about getting their way on taxation. Where the two 'old' parties differ is in that the Old Left is more concerned about maintaining its traditional values than it is about higher taxes, whereas the Old Right is prepared to compromise its stance on social morality in order to maintain its position on taxes.

Against this background, each of the parties has a go at forming a majority government around its own platform. The New Right Party is made up of cheeky upstarts, so they start the bidding. They point out to the New Left and to the Old Right that there is a 65 per cent to 35 per cent majority in favour of the New Right programme over that of the Old Left. A little compromise among the three parties, and they would have a large majority. Yet very quickly the New Left Party points out to the Old Left party that it could avoid the worst of all possible worlds from the Old Left's point of view, namely a government programme with New Right ideas at its core, provided the Old Left would support a programme in which New Left ideas were central. That would give it a majority of 55 per cent to 45 per cent. But then the Old Right points out to the Old Left that the two of them still have a lot in common on issues of social morality and that, with a little compromise, a government programme with Old Right ideas at its core would deliver a parliamentary majority of 75 per cent to 25 per cent. But then the Old Left points out to the New Left that this would be the worst of all possible worlds from its point of view; so why not form a government programme around Old Left ideas, with its 55 per cent to 45 per cent majority? And, just when everyone is getting used to the idea of an Old Left–New Left coalition, the New Right squawks up again: 'Hang on New Left and Old Right, together we can beat a programme that depends on Old Left ideas, since the New Left does not want the Old and the Old Right does not want the Left.'

What has happened? The situation in Folkland's parliament is that any group that looks as if it could form a majority coalition faces an alternative majority coalition that could defeat it. Because any party that is 'out' of some potential governing coalition has an incentive to get 'in' to an alternative coalition, it also has an incentive to encourage some of the present 'ins' to move

Figure 4.1. How Potential Majority Coalitions Cycle

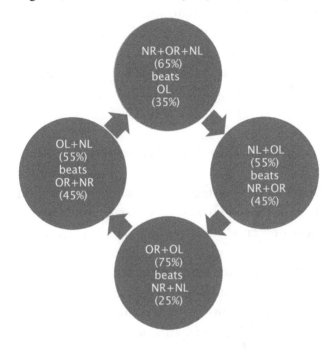

'out' to a new grouping that can form a majority. This is known as a majority rule cycle and is illustrated in Figure 4.1. In this situation, there is no coalition that can form a majority against all other possible coalitions. 'Paper wraps rock, rock blunts scissors, scissors cut paper.' There is no way of ordering paper, rock and scissors such that the distinctive strengths of each triumph over both of the other items. Similarly, in situations where there are alternative political programmes, more than two dimensions of political difference may lead to a situation in which no one coalition can be guaranteed to defeat all the others.

Why These Majorities

It might look as though the parable of Folkland is contrived. However, the sort of political developments* that it illustrates are common across many democratic countries. As new issues make their way onto the political agenda and new generations join the electorate, old alignments break up and new alignments form. Those studying European politics, for example, have noticed that, in addition to the old left–right spectrum in politics, there is now what is called the GAL–TAN spectrum, that is, the green–alternative–libertarian versus traditional–authoritarian–nationalist spectrum. At one time political parties could pitch their appeal on the assumption 'It's the economy, stupid', but that is no longer enough.

When new issues come onto the political agenda, there is a fragmentation of public opinion and no party's stance on the full range of issues a government needs to deal with is likely to be supported by more than a minority of the electorate as a whole. Even when parties form coalitions in government, there will often be a different programme that will be preferred by an alternative majority. In other words, there is always a 'silent majority'. In place of the reasonably satisfying results of the two-party system, the politics of cross-cutting issues is likely to leave a large portion of the electorate increasingly dissatisfied about some issues.

When a portion of the electorate finds itself dissatisfied with prevailing government policy in this way, there is an incentive for new parties to form, or for old parties to reinvent themselves in a new guise, campaigning on those issues where there is dissatisfaction. So, in Europe, populist parties have campaigned against migration and the European Union. Previously the dominant parties in Europe, both on the left and on the right, were pro-European and generally liberal on migration. Yet significant segments of their supporters held contrary views, leaving them open to an electoral appeal by new parties. The French National Front had long campaigned as an anti-immigrant party, but the Euro crisis enabled it also to campaign as a Eurosceptic party that purports to defending working-class jobs. In the United Kingdom UKIP combined its opposition to Europe with its anti-immigrant stance, peeling off Conservative voters in the south and Labour voters in the north of England. In Germany, the Alternative for Germany, which had started life as the 'professors' party' opposed to the single currency, reinvented itself as the anti-immigrant party.

The consequence of all this is that, outside of the very simple situations in which a group of voters are faced with two, and only two, well-defined alternatives, there is no guarantee of there being a majority view. Majority opinion cannot give you the will of the people because you cannot identify an opinion that is clearly the opinion of the majority.

Note that nothing in this argument depends on the assumption that the mass of people in a democracy are ignorant, ill informed or selfish. Quite the opposite, in fact. The logic behind these types of situations was once uncovered by

Lewis Carroll,* the author of *Alice in Wonderland*, after he noted some peculiarities of voting in his Oxford college. Fellows of Oxford colleges are normally thought to be intelligent (or at least think of themselves as intelligent). If the problems of determining a common will can be found in an Oxford college, it can be found anywhere. The will of the people is a myth not because the people are stupid, short-sighted or unwise. It is a myth because you cannot get a single will from a diverse group of people except in the simplest of cases. To suppose that you can is an attempt to square the circle.

A majority rule cycle can arise in any situation in which there is more than one dimension of political disagreement, in particular among highly informed and sophisticated voters such as members of parliamentary parties who have to decide which governing coalition they should join. In fact majority rule cycling is more likely to occur among such experienced voters than among less experienced voters, since those with political experience develop an ability to think of new dimensions of agreement and disagreement when confronted with a choice. Failing to find the will of the people has nothing to do with voter knowledge; it has everything to do with the way in which different and competing opinions can or cannot be combined.

5

The Mythical Sovereign

When the People Choose

Someone who believed in the will of the people could accept all that I have said in the previous chapter, yet still hold that we can meaningfully speak about the will of the people in certain defined situations. Political choice is not always over more than two alternatives. For example, when referendums are held in democracies, the decision usually takes an either/or form. Should there be gay marriage or not? Should religious groups be allowed to put up buildings with minarets? Should a constitutional change be accepted? Whatever the result, you might say that a majority vote expresses the will of the people on the particular questions posed in the referendum. Such cases seem quite different from ones where the choice is over party programmes that each contain a specific combination of policy positions. An either/or choice, as in a referendum, avoids these complications.

For the populist, a referendum is not just a convenient way of reducing complex political matters to a simple either/or choice. Instead, the populist thinks that the use of referendums expresses a deep truth about the character of democracy. This truth is that in a democracy sovereignty belongs to the people. In this way of thinking, the justification for referendums can be captured by three claims. The first is that the people is sovereign. The second is that the people best expresses its will on matters of government policy through direct voting, in a referendum in which a simple majority is decisive. The third is that the function of government is to implement the will of the people as decided by the referendum. As a corollary of these claims, it is said that anything that frustrates the will of the people as expressed in a referendum is simply antidemocratic. When Theresa May declared, at the 2016 Conservative Party conference, that Parliament should not subvert the will of the people as expressed in the Brexit referendum, she was expressing no more and no less than this corollary.

Yet things are not so simple. If the premise on which a referendum is held is the principle of the sovereignty of the people, that idea, taken literally, is a myth.

The Myth of the Sovereign People

Democracy requires the sovereignty of the people. That, at least, is commonly believed. The US constitution starts with the ringing words 'We the People of the United States' and the Irish constitution is declared in the name of 'the people of Eire'. The French constitution begins with a solemn declaration that the French people proclaims its attachment to the rights of man and to the principles of national sovereignty. The opening of Germany's Basic Law says that it has been adopted by the German people exercising its constituent power. The United Kingdom, of course, does not have a constitution contained in a single document, but there are those who say that in its constitution sovereignty has passed from Parliament to the people, though at present the courts do not agree with this claim.

Populists take the idea of the sovereignty of the people literally. In populist thought, the sovereignty of the people means that citizens must be able to exercise direct and decisive control over the making of government policy. Nothing less.

But what is sovereignty? Sovereignty is simply the ability to determine the decision about the meaning and implications of a body of rules. Suppose a dispute arises as to whether a local authority under planning law can prohibit gaming arcades in its town or city. The gaming industry thinks it unlawful; the local authority thinks it lawful. The dispute will work its way up the court system until a final authoritative decision is taken. It may even be necessary for parliament to pass some new legislation to clarify the law. Whoever can make the final determination is the sovereign.

In the days before democracy, the monarch was treated as the sovereign. The king's or queen's will determined what should be done. Much of the history of seventeenth-century England was over the question of whether the king or Parliament had ultimate authority. The English

Civil War was fought over the competition for political power between king and Parliament. And James II was deposed in 1688, his successor accepting the right of Parliament to limit the exercise of the monarch's power. Subsequently, in the nineteenth and twentieth centuries, the vote was extended to a wider range of British subjects, and this created a modern mass democracy.

It seems tempting to tell this story as a tale in which the will of the monarch as sovereign passes to the people, which now possesses its own sovereign will. Tempting, but wrong.* It makes no sense to think of modern democracy as a matter of transferring ultimate authority from the absolute monarch to the people that now occupies the position of that monarch. We cannot intelligibly say that, where once stood the will of the king, there now stands the will of the people. Citizens, as members of a people, cannot give orders to themselves in the same sense in which the monarch gave orders to others. What citizens can do is participate in political processes by which laws are made and policies adopted. Citizens can vote, can lobby their MP, can support organizations that pursue political aims, can protest, can join political parties, can present evidence to Parliament, can challenge the government in the courts – and so on. What they cannot do is govern themselves by making the laws they are to obey. They cannot do this, not because they lack the capacity to think intelligently about law and policy, but because the making of law and policy requires procedures and institutions established through constitutional rules, rules about how law and policy can validly be made. A government's authority for making law and policy depends on those constitutional rules. This is why the principle of the rule of law is a central value in a democracy. Constitutional rules define the powers and authority of different actors in the political system.

We can make the same point by contrasting how a sovereign monarch can govern and how popular government can work. Imagine a sovereign monarch whose word is law. What he or she says goes. Courtiers are ready to do the monarch's bidding and, by a combination of military force and popular resignation, that will is put into practice. Laws are passed, taxes raised and foreign wars fought. Now imagine that the people are performing the same function. The people have to decide what laws are passed, what taxes are raised and what wars are fought. The trouble is obvious. The monarch could speak with one voice. The people speaks with many. Out of the different views on government policy that individuals and groups have, there has to emerge one common course of action. The voice of *the* people has to be distilled from the voices of people. The wills of many have to become one. But, before they can become one, there have to be rules for defining the way in which the different voices are reconciled; and people cannot do this for themselves.

If this is true, how is it that constitutions so often declare themselves in the name of the people? When the American constitution, for example, announces itself as being proclaimed by 'We the People', how are we to understand this claim? The answer is: certainly not by imagining that the whole of the American people actually wrote the constitution. The original constitutional document was not written by the people, but by delegates to the constitutional convention held in Philadelphia in the hot summer of 1787. In fact those delegates had exceeded their authority, since they had been charged by the Congress of the original thirteen states merely with revising the existing Articles of Confederation. Nevertheless, the Congress decided that the new constitution could be presented for ratification, to state conventions specially chosen for the purpose. Rhode Island, which had originally failed to ratify the constitution through a referendum, later ratified it through a state convention. In short, when the authors of the constitution proclaimed it in the name of 'We the People', they were anticipating some measure of popular support gained through elected conventions; they were not acting as the scribes of some preexisting will of the people.

In any case, there is an interesting question as to what the framers understood by 'the people' when they drew up the constitution.* If they were thinking of electors, then only a minority of individuals living in America at the time would have been included. Women, children and chattel slaves were excluded from the electorate, which was made up of free adult males, themselves subject to property or income tests. When they thought of individuals for such things as census purposes, they notoriously decided that slaves only counted as three-fifth persons. In other words their understanding fell way short of how we would nowadays define a people. The reason why they presented the constitution as emanating from 'We the People' seems to be that they wanted to detach the ratification process from the existing political institutions of the thirteen states. But they certainly did not think that anything like the opinions of the whole of the adult population should decide political matters in general.

This conclusion may make it seem as though the framers were trying to pull some sort of confidence trick, pretending to speak in the name of the people while being a political elite. But this is the only way in which a new democratic constitution can be formed: first the authors have to write it and then they have to present it for acceptance – either to the people at large, in a referendum, or to its representatives. Either way no people literally authors its own constitution.

But if the people is not sovereign in any straightforward sense, it can still be true that, by exercising its powers under a constitution that establishes referendums, the people is more in control than it is when its representatives take important political decisions. Rousseau once said that British people thought they were free, but they were wrong; they were free only once every five years, when they elected their representatives. Can the people not be free more often if it can govern through referendums?

The Question How

Suppose you get on the bathroom scales one day and, as a result, you decide that you definitely have to lose some weight. You say to yourself, in as stern a voice as you can muster: 'Take some action to lose weight!'. You seem to have decided something. But is that true? What precisely have you decided to do? You know that you want to shed some fat but, until you adopt a feasible plan as to how to achieve that goal, you cannot act on your self-instruction. Do you get off the commuter train one stop early and walk the rest of the way to work? Do you buy a cross-trainer? Do you take out a gym club subscription? Or do you just try to cut down on croissants and lattes? Until you answer these questions, you cannot set yourself a feasible plan. You need to know the 'how' as well as the 'what'. If you remain stuck at the 'what' spot, you are really in a 'not' spot. You might as well never have made the resolution in the first place. At least you will save yourself the guilty feelings when you fail to put your resolution into practice. The guiding principle here is found in the words of the old song, 'It ain't what you do, it's the way that you do it. That's what gets results.'

The same principle applies to referendums. How the referendum is conducted is crucial. The first problem is how the referendum question is phrased. The case for saying that a majority vote in a referendum represents the will of the people depends on the question's taking a simply either/or form. Yet political alternatives are seldom simple either/or choices – and this for a number of reasons. Given that the world is complex, any alternative will still be only a partial description of what is on offer, specifying some but not all consequences of the decision. A vote in favour of gay marriage may create a situation in which heterosexual couples have no legal opportunity for civil unions, whereas gay couples can choose between a civil partnership and a marriage. A vote against the construction of buildings with minarets may still leave open the question of what is to happen to buildings that already have minarets. Should they be pulled down or allowed to stand? A vote in favour of a constitutional change, say, a change to elect a president directly rather than through Parliament, still leaves open questions about the term of office, the qualifications for being a presidential candidate, or how a president might be removed in case of malfeasance in office.

But this is not simply a question of the incomplete description of any one alternative. A further problem is who selects what alternatives are put up for referendum. Recall the citizens of Folkland and their political divisions. On issues to do with social morality – gay marriage, physician-assisted dying, drug use – they would usually vote on the conservative side. By contrast, on questions to do with the development and expansion of the welfare state – funding for social care, parental leave for those with newborn children, or worker health and safety – they would usually vote on the left-wing side. If only the issues about social morality are put up for decision by referendum, then the will of the people is being distorted, since only one dimension of its total views is being considered.

The problem here is with what political scientists call agenda setting. Referendums do not simply happen. They have to be organized, questions have to be formulated and alternatives defined. How the agenda is set matters; and, if it is set by the government, then the government is setting the agenda. But what if people set the agenda themselves? A referendum run as a popular initiative is one in which the questions to be put to the vote come from citizens rather than from the government of the day. Would the popular initiative not be an expression of the will of the people? You might think that popular initiatives avoid the problem of agenda setting, but unfortunately this is not so. There can be manipulation through sections of the population placing different initiatives on the agenda.

Consider just one example in Arizona,* a US state that provides for the popular initiative. In 1990 there were two proposals to establish a state holiday for Martin Luther King Day. One proposal kept the same number of paid holidays as then existed and eliminated Columbus Day as a paid holiday. The second kept Columbus Day, and hence added to the number of paid holidays. The effect of these two proposals was that those who favoured making Martin Luther King Day a paid holiday would spit their vote between the two propositions. In effect, what might seem to be a simple either/or choice around the question of whether there should be a Martin Luther King Day holiday became a three-way choice: the status quo, with no such holiday; the holiday without Columbus Day; and the holiday with Columbus Day. If you wish to frustrate the proposal for there to be a Martin Luther King Day holiday, then propose an alternative that is close enough to the original to siphon off some of the support for the proposal. Splitting the opposition is an old principle of politics. Having a popular initiative does not prevent that tactic from being used, and therefore cannot provide a sure-fire way of finding the will of the people.

6

On Being Outnumbered

In a Minority

Suppose everything so far in this book is wrong. Suppose that, when we talk about 'the people' in a democracy, we are referring to citizens who identify with their country without reservation: they genuinely form one collective body. Suppose the political choice those citizens face can be neatly divided into two alternatives, with no complications about third, fourth and other possibilities. Suppose that a clear majority has chosen one of the two alternatives. Suppose, too, that the government acts in good faith, conducting itself as a loyal servant of the people, seeking to implement the will of the majority as best it can and without distortion. What follows?

A common answer is that those in the minority should bend their wills to the will of the majority. If a choice is made by the majority of the people, who am I to challenge that choice? Is it not undemocratic to do so? Exactly the opposite is true. If you are in a minority and you genuinely and sincerely believe that the majority has made a mistake, then you not only have a right to continue to oppose the decision, you have a duty to do so. To say that someone has a right is to say what he or she is permitted to do. By contrast, a duty is like an instruction. If someone says to you that you have a duty to do something, then that person's claim is that you must do it. To say that you have a duty to oppose a majority decision is to say that you must oppose a majority decision if you believe that serious damage to the common good would result from implementing that decision. When Churchill opposed appeasement in the 1930s, he was in a minority. The vast majority of people wanted to avoid a repeat of the horrors of the First World War. Churchill thought that he had a duty to continue to warn against appeasement. In the end he turned out to be right. To oppose the majority is not a crime; and in some cases it can be a duty.

At this point, once again, Rousseau haunts the discussion. Rousseau thought that, when you were outvoted, you should realize that you have mistaken the general will and simply accept that you were wrong. If everyone is voting in sincere pursuit of the general will, then it is the majority that is right. If you are in the minority, you should realize that you have not found the general will.

Is there any reason for believing that being in a minority is a sign that you are wrong? Yes, there is, and it is based on the mathematics of probability. Such a reason is given by what is known as the jury theorem.* This theorem assumes that a group of people who are making a political choice is like a jury that has to decide as a matter of fact whether someone is innocent or guilty. To illustrate the theorem, we can consider any group of people that has to determine a common course of action on the basis of their individual judgements as to what is correct or incorrect.

Outnumbered and Mistaken?

Imagine that three friends like walking together and they get a lot of fun from practising the art of walking by reading the signs of nature. Using their understanding of rock formations, lichen on trees, or the movement of streams and rivers, they aim to walk from one place to another by the quickest route, without using maps or mobile phones. Each is experienced in this sort of walking and, when asked to choose one of two possible paths, they usually do a good job of finding the quicker one. In fact, each tends to be correct about 60 per cent of the time. Each one, then, has an equal chance of being correct, and this chance is better than even. In this sense, they are all biased; but it is a good bias to have, since they incline to making the correct decision.

Given this bias in the choices that individuals make, what is the chance that a majority decision will be correct? Mathematically it can be shown that the chance that majorities are correct is higher than the chance that any one of the individuals is correct.

To see why, consider a specific problem that our three friends might face. Suppose they have been walking all day and they are now looking for the quickest way to their destination. They come to a fork in the road, one path leading left and another leading right. Suppose that the leftward path is the quicker one. Given that the leftward path is quicker, each has a 60 per cent chance of choosing it. Given that the rightward path is the incorrect choice, each has a 40 per cent chance of choosing that path. (Remember that, when making the choice, they do not know whether the correct path is left or right.)

What is the chance that a majority will make the correct decision? To work this out we must use the rule of joint probabilities. Joint probabilities can be illustrated by what is known in horse racing as an accumulator bet. In an accumulator bet money is placed on a horse in one race and the winnings, if there is any, are placed on horses in subsequent races. In a treble bet, for example, if one pound is placed on a horse at 10 to 1 and the horse wins, then £10 will be placed on a second horse, and then, if that horse wins, the winnings will be placed on a third horse. If all three horses have odds of 10 to 1 and all three win, then the person betting £1 on the first horse will earn £1,000 when the third horse comes in.

What is the chance of winning £1,000? It is the chance of each horse winning multiplied by the chances of the other horses winning. We simply multiply the individual probabilities. If the odds are fair – which means, if there really is a 1 in 10 chance that each horse wins – then the probability of wining the treble bet is 1 in 1,000 (0.1 × 0.1 × 0.1), or one tenth of one per cent (0.1%) if you express the figure as a percentage.

The logic of the jury theorem works on the same principle of joint probabilities. Return to our three friends. To assess the joint probabilities of their making the correct decision, we need to work out all the possible ways in which they might reach their majority judgement. There are two paths to choose from, and there are three friends. Logically there are eight possible ways in which the choices of three individuals can combine over two options. All might choose the left path or all might choose the right. We can treat both these situations as cases of coming to a majority decision (three votes to zero). Alternatively, two might choose the left path and one the right. Or two might choose the right path and one the left. These possible combinations are displayed in Table 6.1.

Table 6.1. The Possible Combinations of Choice

Possible Combinations	A	B	C	Majority Choice	Chance Majority Correct
Possibility 1	Left	Left	Left	Left	21.6%
Possibility 2	Left	Left	Right	Left	14.4%
Possibility 3	Left	Right	Left	Left	14.4%
Possibility 4	Right	Left	Left	Left	14.4%
Possibility 5	Right	Right	Left	Right	9.6%
Possibility 6	Right	Left	Right	Right	9.6%
Possibility 7	Left	Right	Right	Right	9.6%
Possibility 8	Right	Right	Right	Right	6.4%

What is the chance that a majority will choose the correct path, given that each individual is more likely to choose the correct path than the incorrect path? Using our rule of joint probabilities, we can work this out for each possible combination of choice. For example, in the first combination, the chance that all three are right is

21.6 per cent (0.6 × 0.6 × 0.6, expressed as a percentage). Similarly, if only A and B choose the left path, which is the correct path, then the chance that they, as a majority, will be right is 14.4 per cent (0.6 × 0.6 × 0.4, expressed as a percentage) – and so on down all the possible combinations.

Looking at Table 6.1 it is clear that the chance for any one majority to be correct and choose the leftward path is higher than the chance for the majority to be wrong and take the rightward path. In addition, the chance that all the majority possibilities are correct is higher than the chance that they are incorrect and higher than the chance that any one individual is correct. It seems that a majority decision is not only a convenient way to resolve a difference of opinion but is also more like to lead to the correct decision.

There is a further twist to the tale. If we increase the number of voting individuals, the chance for a combination to hit on the right answer increases as well – to the point where, with a very large number of individuals, it is virtually certain that such a combination will occur. It seems that Rousseau might have been correct when he said that the will of the majority tends to be right. If so, are you not obliged to change your mind and admit you are wrong if you are in a minority?

Impressive as this argument is, it does not carry the strong implications that some imagine. Its significance depends on how plausible the underlying assumptions are. In particular, the mathematics is identical if we assume that each person has an equal and better than even chance of choosing incorrectly. For example, if there is a 60 per cent chance that people choose incorrectly, then the chance that majorities choose incorrectly is 64.8 per cent. The mathematics follows the assumptions that we make about how likely people are to be right when they choose.

More fundamentally, important political choices are not like our three friends trying to choose the correct path. They had an agreed end, and the only question was how best to get there. In political choices there is disagreement about the ends as well as about the means. Some people want an open and liberal society even at the cost of some social disorder, whereas others want a stable and conformist society even at the cost of intolerance. Some people are prepared to allow for greater economic inequality in order to promote entrepreneurship, whereas others favour greater equality even if there is less wealth to spread around. The jury theorem only applies when you think that a political choice can be shown to be straightforwardly correct or incorrect. Most of us recognize when we vote that there is something to be said on both sides of a question and that what we are trying to do is to come to a conclusion that we think is reasonable, not straightforwardly correct or incorrect.

Often in practical politics you cannot delay making a decision. In that case, majority decision-making is reasonable, not because it is more likely to be correct than incorrect, but because it is a fair way of dealing with differences of judgement if a choice cannot be postponed or made to await further discussion. Decisions made through agreed democratic procedures have authority. This is a reason for not trying illegally to frustrate the policy. But it is not a reason to bend your will to the will of the majority or to correct your judgement if you conscientiously and sincerely hold a contrary view. Indeed, if you think that the majority is mistaken, you have a duty, as a citizen, to continue to oppose that policy in the best way you can, using all the democratic rights at your disposal.

The Duty to Oppose

Suppose that there is a major issue of public policy that has gone to a referendum in a country. If you are a citizen of the country that has voted in the referendum, if you thought long and hard about the issue at stake before the referendum, seeking to establish the relevant facts and coming to a judgement as to which way to vote, if it turns out that you are in a minority, and if you also think that the majority decision is damaging to the common good of your country – then you have a duty to oppose the result.

Why? As a member of a democratic society, you not only enjoy rights, you also have responsibilities. Those responsibilities include making your contribution to the understanding of what government policies are required for the common good. You need to educate yourself about the issues to be decided and you need to listen and respond to others. You need to care about the integrity of the public realm, supporting the maintenance of high standards of public broadcasting and social communication. When you take sides, as eventually you must, you need to do so with modesty and with the courage of your convictions. In short, when we try to live on the right terms with others, we make our contribution to our society by taking seriously the demands of the common good and the plurality of reasonable views it contains.

When assessing the duty to oppose a policy, it does not matter whether the decision was taken by a referendum, by parliament, or by president and Congress. To see why not, consider any controversial piece of legislation passed in accordance with the constitution of the country. In the United Kingdom for example, consider the legislation that settled the community charge, which was passed in 1988. This legislation established a new form of local government finance, according to which every adult resident in a local authority area would be required to pay the same tax towards local services as everyone else. Since residential status was based on the names that appeared on the electoral register, this was in effect a poll tax, a tax on the right to vote. The legislation was controversial because it obviously meant that the poor would pay as much as the rich in taxation. As people said at the time, the duke and the dustman living in the same area would pay the same.

Yet, although this legislation was controversial (and, in my view, was wrong), there is no doubt that it was passed by due constitutional process. It was a proposal that had appeared in the Conservative Party manifesto of 1987. That election produced a Conservative landslide of 376 MPs (only twenty-one down on their numbers in 1983) with a popular vote of 43.4 per cent, which was up from their popular vote of 42.4 per cent in 1983. So the government could claim an electoral mandate for the proposal. The measure went through the proper parliamentary procedures and received royal assent on 29 July 1988.

Suppose that someone suggested in 1988, when the legislation was passed, that there was no longer any right to oppose it, because the legislation had been made by a duly authorized act of parliament with a popular mandate. Then citizens who took their democratic responsibilities seriously would not have been entitled to engage in the campaigns that led to the repeal of the legislation some two years later. But, of course, opposing the legislation was not undemocratic, and the reason why this is so is quite simple. When parliament passed the legislation, it made a mistake, but it took the campaigning of those opposed to the poll tax to rectify the mistake.

Referendums cannot bind more tightly than can the legislation of parliament. A fundamental principle of parliamentary democracy is that no parliament can bind its successors. Parliament may pass a law one year and repeal it the following year without any loss of authority. Just as parliament at one time cannot bind its successors at a later time, so no referendum can be seen as a permanent expression of popular will. The only way of assessing permanence in the will of the people would be to hold referendums on the same issue at repeated intervals, for example once in a decade. It is no use invoking the will of the people from one referendum in order to prevent a reversal of that decision in a later referendum. There is no mythical body of 'the people' behind the individuals who make up the electorate at any one time. And, as long as that is true, there is always a right, and sometimes a duty, to continue to oppose a majority vote in a referendum with which you disagree.

7

Democracy without Myth

The Mirage of Populism

Populism creates mirages. Mirages appear to have substance, but on inspection they turn out to be an illusion. Populists think that the problem with modern government is that it is not directly run by the people. But there are no examples of government by popular assembly that could serve as models for such a form of government in the modern state. Government by assembly in ancient Athens was government by a fraction of the citizens, who represented in turn a fraction of the total population. Rousseau imagined citizens as sharing a simple life and spontaneously coordinating their actions, an image as false as it is useless in guiding contemporary thinking about democratic reform. Government by popular assembly does survive at the town level in Switzerland, in some New England communities, and elsewhere; but it is limited to local affairs. It comes nowhere near the major areas of government policy that are so central to the well-being of the citizens of a modern state: economic policy, national education, healthcare, transport, protection of the environment, international trade, defence and foreign policy.

Populism alleges that the corruption and ills of representative democracy would be rectified if the will of the people prevailed in policy. Yet, as a doctrine, populism must ultimately fail because it is built on a myth – the myth of the will of the people. The will of the people is a myth because the assumptions that are necessary to make it a reality cannot be realized in the world of politics. First, we can give no simple meaning to the idea of 'the people' or of 'a people' forming a state. Thought of as a body of individual citizens, the people is made up of many who have diverse views and opinions. Often these diverse views and opinions stem from the historical experiences of different groups incorporated through processes of modern state building. Do the citizens of the United Kingdom form a people, or are there different peoples in the United Kingdom – the English, the Scots, the Welsh and the Irish? What position you take on such questions is a matter of political choice as much as anything else; it certainly does not represent some natural fact about the world. Even if a state contains one and only one people or nation, it contains many different people – individuals and their families, with different and sometimes competing interests and opinions.

These differences of opinion make for complex cross-currents in political alignments. At some times and in some countries, it made sense to think of political competition as taking place between two parties, one on the left and the other on the right. This way of thinking could without too much distortion be applied to the United Kingdom between 1945 and 1975 and to the United States for at least the early part of the same period, as well as to some other countries, for instance New Zealand. Even at the time, the two-party system suppressed some important political issues, most obviously environmental protection. Private affluence can be combined with public squalor, as politics in the immediate postwar period showed. If both of your major parties are focused on growing the pie as quickly as possible, they will pay little attention to the quality of air, rivers, soils and seas. Two-party politics also suppressed other issues. In the United States the politics of race was taken off the political agenda for much of the mid-twentieth century, as the question of what to do about segregation was corralled inside the uneasy truce of northern and southern Democrats. When Lyndon Johnson's civil rights legislation was passed, Johnson knew he had lost large parts of the South for the Democrats.

The stable, boring politics of two-party competition for the centre voter, side-lining some issues, has been broken apart through the creation of new forces that focus on the politics of race, gender, the environment and social morality. In turn, mobilization around these issues has caused a counter-revolution led by nationalist and morally conservative forces. The chief effect of these changes has been to fragment the old alignments that once split populations into two large political camps, and also to make it virtually impossible for any one party to formulate principles and establish a programme that appeals to the majority of citizens.

The myth of the will of the people fosters another mirage. It can lead to a politics in which the government pretends to have a direct relationship with the people while always controlling the questions that are put to the popular vote. If there are no constitutional principles governing when a referendum can and cannot be called, then the government controls the occasions when the voice of the people is expressed. How and in what way a referendum result is implemented is also in the hands of government, not of the people. In trying to take back control, the people creates just the conditions in which control becomes lodged in the governing party. The governing party substitutes itself for the people.

One people; one will; one choice. This is the slogan of those who use the will of the people to silence their opponents. It embodies an attitude that is about as far as you can get from the authentic principles of democracy. If we give up the idea of the will of the people, we do not give up on those principles. We need democracy without myth.

Democracy without Myth

Politics is for the genuine many, not the imaginary one. Politics requires plural voices,* not singular orthodoxies. 'Why, oh why, can't politicians agree?' is a regular complaint. Sometimes what this really means is 'Why, oh why, can't politicians agree with me?' If that is what the question means, the answer is simple: if they agreed with you, they would be disagreeing with someone else. The plural voices of politics are not a curse to be eliminated, but the consequence of people's exercising their minds and reason in conditions of freedom. We have elections and referendums so that practical policy decisions can be made. We have freedom of speech and political association so that, when those elections and referendums take place, all citizens have the opportunity to hear different points of view, consider their significance and decide accordingly.

Because there are plural voices in politics, public opinion fragments. If we go back to Folkland, we can see that there was no obvious majority once citizens had identified four political positions. In that situation, some can argue that the largest block should count as the majority; others can argue that any coalition of parties with a majority in the legislature on the basis of a common programme is the majority; and yet others can argue that the true way of determining what the majority favours is to consider majorities on an issue-by-issue basis. These three ways of understanding majority rule correspond to three ways of thinking about government and parliament.

Those who believe it best to identify the single largest group with the majority typically favour the Westminster system of government. In the United Kingdom, the first-past-the-post electoral system with its one-member constituencies works to magnify the presence of two leading parties in parliament. Correspondingly, it reduces the presence of parties in the House of Commons that represent minority currents of opinion, unless those parties, for instance the Scottish National Party or the parties in Northern Ireland, campaign in geographically concentrated areas. In consequence, one of the two large parties is likely to be able to form a single party government, while the other large party forms the opposition. This happens despite the fact that no one party since 1935 has secured a majority of the popular vote. None of the Thatcher governments in the

1980s, for example, secured as much as 44 per cent of the popular vote.

For supporters of the Westminster system, however, it is sufficient to treat the single largest block as the majority because the system delivers clear and accountable government. Because one party can normally form the government, it is clear who is in charge and it is clear who can be blamed if things go wrong. Since relatively small swings in public opinion can lead to large shifts in the seats gained by the two leading parties over time, the 'ins' will become 'outs' and the 'outs' 'ins'. This alternation in government is what is supposed to make the system democratic.

Single-party government is supposed to be strong and stable government. But by the same token it is also government that can make large blunders, unconstrained by the need to compromise with voices that contest the policy. The poll tax could be passed only because there was one party that controlled the government and its leadership could exercise discipline over MPs.

By contrast, if you have a view that says that you have a democratically representative government only when the parties that form the government reflect a majority of the popular vote, then you are naturally driven to favour coalition government of the type found in Germany or Austria. In these systems, governing parties have a majority in parliament and sometimes a large majority of support among the electorate, particularly when the government is formed by a 'grand coalition' of the two largest parties. For example, in Germany in 2013 the governing parties, made out of the Christian and the Social Democratic parties, represented around two thirds of the electorate.

Such a system secures majority rule in one sense, but not in others. As we saw in the case of Folkland, a governing coalition may represent a majority, but it is possible that an alternative majority might have formed instead. To say that a government is a majority coalition government is not to say that it is the only majority coalition government that might have formed, given the constellation of political forces at the time.

The third vision of majority rule is the one that corresponds to the issue-by-issue majority principle. In this version of majority rule, governing parties do not have a majority of votes in parliament but are maintained in office by some opposition parties that do not take government office. In this situation the governing parties do not expect to secure all their policy goals, but policies are decided by shifting majorities in parliament. For example, Danish governments typically rest on a minority of seats in parliament, but can allow policies to be decided by shifting majorities of the parliamentary vote. Similarly, minority Scottish National Party governments in Scotland have legislated through shifting majorities. This situation can arise even in Westminster, as Theresa May discovered in 2017, when the election she called led to the Conservatives' losing their overall majority. The government has been granted 'confidence and supply' by the Democratic Unionists, without the implication that it is entitled to secure the whole – or even a major part – of its programme.

If someone asks 'Which is the true form of majority government among these three alternatives?', the honest answer is that the question is meaningless. Such a question assumes that, amid the plurality of different opinions, there is an underlying real majority opinion. But usually there is not. What we consider to be the majority view depends upon the way we define 'majority' and upon the rules that are used to combine different political opinions together. In other words, what counts as a majority is in part a matter of convention. A convention has the characteristic that it could be other than it is. In many parts of the world people nod their heads when they mean 'yes' and they shake their heads when they mean 'no'. But in other parts of the world the reverse holds: nodding your head means 'no' and shaking your head means 'yes'. It makes no sense to ask which way of moving your head is the right way to say 'yes' or 'no'. This depends on the prevailing convention. Conventions can be changed, but they can only be changed for other conventions.

In consequence, we can say that a majority is the single largest group, or a coalition of groups that forms an absolute majority, or the shifting majorities that form when votes are taken on particular issues. Despite the element of convention, the definition of majority rule is not arbitrary. It is not just a case of anything goes. But more than one thing might go. As it happens, I think there is a lot to be said for thinking of majority government in terms of issue-by-issue voting, because this allows for free association of opinion, which is an important value in a democracy.

Others, by contrast, place great value on accountability and clarity in government. They say that you cannot have government accountable to the population at large when the policies adopted by governments are the result of ad hoc and shifting coalitions. These are at least two reasonable, but competing, points of view.

It is perfectly compatible with recognizing these differences to say that prevailing conventions, even if you disagree with them, can rightly form the basis on which policy is made. What you cannot say is that, when policies are made according to one of these conventions, the government is acting according to the will of the people even when it is acting in accordance with the majority view, for what would count as the majority view would be different under a different convention.

A Place for Referendums?

It might seem, from what I have argued so far, that there is no place for referendums in a democratic society. If we are sceptical about the will of the people, should we not also be sceptical about what is sometimes regarded as the principal method for ascertaining the will of the people? To answer this question, much depends on the form that a referendum takes. Are we thinking of plebiscites, constitutional referendums, popular initiatives, or ad hoc referendums? Referendums take different forms.*

Plebiscites are typical of presidential regimes in which the president calls a referendum in order to rise above the clash of political parties in the legislature and to strengthen executive power. For example, in France, General de Gaulle, as president, used a plebiscite to resolve the political crisis in Algeria in 1961, as well as gaining a mandate from French electors to create the new Fifth Republic in 1958. De Gaulle was at least true to his convictions; for, when he lost the referendum of 1969, he resigned. However, in the general run of cases, particularly in Latin America, the plebiscite is used by the president to cement personal rule – that is, the claim to embody the higher interest of the nation over the claims of contending political parties.

We can contrast the presidential plebiscite with the constitutional referendum. Some countries, such as Ireland, regularly use referendums on important constitutional matters without this centralizing the power in the executive. The Irish constitution requires in Article 46(2) that any proposal for an amendment of the constitution be submitted to the people in a referendum for approval. Such referendums arguably serve to check the executive power, particularly on matters such as European treaties, by contrast with presidential plebiscites. And, on the question of gay marriage, a referendum was probably the only way in which the Irish could resolve their political differences.

Popular initiatives are variants on the referendum in which any section of the population can introduce a question for political decision. They are at the opposite end of the spectrum from the presidential plebiscite; and they respect the principle that the agenda for decision is a consequence of what some citizens think important. They are particularly characteristic of Switzerland and a number of states in the United States.

It might be thought that the use of the popular initiative made a society more democratic, but this need not be true. It is hard to argue, for example, that Switzerland is a more democratic society than Germany. Although the former relies on the principle of the popular initiative and the latter does not, we cannot infer from this that the former is also the more democratic. One of the reasons why we cannot draw this conclusion is that turn-out in elections is higher in Germany than in Switzerland. Since 1949, the lowest general election turnout in Germany has been just over 70 per cent in 2009 and the highest just over 90 per cent in 1972. By contrast, in Switzerland, the average turnout over the last forty-four elections and referendums is less than 50 per cent. There is a difference between the democratic opportunities that a country offers and the extent to which those opportunities are taken up. A high take-up of relatively few opportunities may be better than a low take-up of relatively frequent opportunities.

The basic case for holding a referendum is that there are some issues that arise on the political agenda of societies that cannot realistically be handled through the normal processes of contest among political parties. Existential issues that change the standing and status of the country typically fall into this category. Extensions to the power of the European Union or secession are two obvious examples. Even in these cases, however, depending on history and tradition, referendums are not always the answer. The popular initiative provides opportunities; but of itself it does not improve the quality of democracy unless those opportunities are taken up.

What, then, of the ad hoc referendums? These can occur in political systems like that of the United Kingdom, which have neither the constitutional provision of Ireland nor the routine frequency of systems with a popular initiative. There is little to be said for referendums in these circumstances. They have the arbitrariness of the presidential plebiscite without the virtue of the routine popular initiative. They may solve problems within political parties, as did the 1975 and 2016 EU referendums in the United Kingdom, but only at the cost of creating constitutional uncertainty.

Even if we say that an ad hoc referendum gives a government a mandate to carry out the will of the people, what happens when circumstances change and unforeseen events occur – in other words, always? Unlike parliaments, the people is neither in permanent session nor available for emergency recalls. The negotiation and compromise that is at the heart of good legislation and policy is not something that can be conducted by the people. This is not to say that negotiation and compromise are always done well by parliaments. It is to say that only representative bodies are capable of attending to detail and circumstance.

8

The Ethics of Responsibility

Populism alleges that the corruption and ills of representative democracy would be rectified if the will of the people prevailed in policy. In its UK form, the myth of populism has gathered around the Brexit referendum. Judge the will of the people by a popular referendum. Insist that all those who continue to oppose the result of the referendum are opposing the will of the people. Make conformity to the supposed will of the people the test of society's democratic credentials. Keep repeating this stale formula. Be intolerant of dissent. Challenge the constitutional constraints of the courts and parliament. Allow the bully boys of the press to reinforce the message through attacks on opponents. One people; one will; one party.

Today the dangers of democracy come from within. Democracies are now endangered by policies adopted supposedly in the name of democracy. Political parties that secure a temporary majority in the legislature may easily start to dismantle the guardrails of democracy:* the authority of the constitutional courts, the process of appointment to public office, the political independence of the media, the standing of expert independent bodies, the standing of the professions, the right of governments other than central government to shape public policy, the role of trades unions.

The problems that democracies face these days are serious. If anyone thinks that the effective regulation of finance, the control of cross-border monopolies, the protection of the environment, the decent education of children, the provision of universal healthcare, the financing of social security, the humane response to refugees and asylum seekers, the guarantee of defence from external attack or a host of other problems are easy, then they should think again. No democratic purpose is served by pretending that things are simpler than they are. No good is achieved by asserting that the problems can all be solved by appeal to the will of the people.

The opposite of myth is reality: things as they are. T. S. Eliot once wrote: 'Human kind cannot bear very much reality.'* This is not only bad poetry but a false motto for the open societies that democracies should be. In my experience at least, the citizens of democracies want decent behaviour from those who govern them and honesty about what governments can do. They do not want fairy tales. They do not expect to live in a society in which the lion lays down with the lamb and swords are beaten into ploughshares.

The responsible exercise of power means thinking hard about the consequences of policy and dealing honestly with objections. It requires making a virtue of the pluralism that lies at the heart of politics, not turning that pluralism into a vice. When politicians shirk that task and invoke the will of the people as justification for their policies without engaging with the substance of policy argument, you know that they have lost their sense of responsibility.

As I write, parliament is still exercising its powers over crucial pieces of legislation connected with Brexit. That is as it should be. The High Court judgement of 3 November 2016 was a beautifully written exposition of the principles of parliamentary sovereignty, the rule of law and the limits of government by executive decree. As the Court pointed out, fundamental to the principle of parliamentary democracy is the idea that a government can only exercise its powers by the authority of parliament. The rule of law is needed to ensure that the powers claimed by governments have democratic authorization.

Populism is the sigh of the oppressed creature. Any democratic system worthy of the name will respond to that sigh. But it should respond not on the basis of myth, but on the basis of a realistic assessment of alternatives. Realism is not the same as resignation. Things as they are is not the same as things as they might be. Realism does not mean giving up on serious social and economic reform. It does mean recognizing that responsible politics is about deciding on the basis of the wills of different people, not the mythical ghost that supposedly animates the body of a singular people.

Notes and Sources

Yet, despite this diversity, the term 'populist' (p. 4): see Cas Mudde and Cristóbal Rovira Kaltwasser, *Populism: A Very Short Introduction* (Oxford: Oxford University Press, 2017), ch. 1.

infantile within the sphere of his real interests (p. 7): Joseph Schumpeter, *Capitalism, Socialism and Democracy* [1943], with an introduction by Richard Swedberg (London: Routledge, 1994), p. 262.

systematic ignorance (p. 7): for proposals to have test qualifications for voting, see Jason Brennan, *Against Democracy* (Princeton, NJ: Princeton University Press, 2016), ch. 8.

Between 1980 and 2016 (p. 9): for these figures, see the *World Inequality Report 2018*, available at http://wir2018.wid.world (accessed 7 January 2018).

Viktor Orbán (p. 13): see Jan-Werner Müller, *What Is Populism?* (Penguin: Kindle edition, 2017), p. 26.

the original and most influential image of direct democracy (p. 19): for example, see James S. Fishkin, *The Voice of the People: Public Opinion and Democracy* (New Haven, CT: Yale University Press, 1995) p. 18.

Pericles (p. 19): the translation of this passage comes from Thucydides, *History of the Peloponnesian War*, translated by Rex Warner, with an introduction and notes by M. I. Finley (Harmondsworth: Penguin, 1954), p. 147.

'what all have already 'felt' (book 4, ch. 1) (p. 26): quotation from Jean-Jacques Rousseau, *The Social Contract*, translated with an introduction by G. D. H. Cole (London: J. M. Dent & Sons, 1973), p. 247. (Quotation repeated here in chapter 4, p. 47.)

a small and isolated Swiss agricultural community called Törbel (p. 27): see Robert McC. Netting, *Balancing on an Alp: Ecological Change and Continuity in a Swiss Mountain Community* (Cambridge: Cambridge University Press, 1981).

the heartland (p. 35): the idea of the heartland is taken from Paul Taggart, *Populism* (Buckingham: Open University Press, 2000).

In 1854, a guide to the Mézenc region (p. 36): on the remoteness of the region, see Graham Robb, *The Discovery of France* (Basingstoke: Picador, 2007), pp. 3–5.

turning peasants into Frenchmen (p. 37): allusion to the title of Eugen Weber, *Peasants into Frenchmen:*

The Modernization of Rural France 1870–1914 (London: Chatto & Windus, 1977).

a process of making Americans (p. 41): for an excellent account, see Desmond King, *Making Americans: Immigration, Race, and the Origins of the Diverse Democracy* (Cambridge, MA: Harvard University Press, 2000).

the *only* rule that has these qualities (p. 50): for those who want the formal logic behind this statement, the key result is Kenneth O. May, 'A Set of Independent, Necessary and Sufficient Conditions for Simple Majority Decision', *Econometrica* 20 (1952): 680–4.

'boring politics is the price that contented voters pay for reasonably satisfying results' (p. 52): I take this splendid phrase from an outstanding study of the transformation of New Zealand politics in the late twentieth century: Jack Nagel, 'Social Choice in a Pluritarian Democracy', *British Journal of Political Science* 28.2 (1998): 223–67, here p. 263.

the sort of political developments (p. 62): these are succinctly presented in Herbert Kitschelt, 'Popular Dissatisfaction with Democracy: Populism and Party Systems', in Yves Mény and Yves Surel, eds, *Democracies and the Populist Challenge* (Basingstoke: Macmillan, 2002), pp. 179–96, an article that summarizes Kitschelt's informative research.

Lewis Carroll (p. 65): his papers are reprinted in Duncan Black, *The Theory of Committees and*

Elections (Cambridge: Cambridge University Press, 1958), and more recently in Duncan Black, *The Theory of Committees and Elections*, edited I. McLean et al. (Boston, MA: Kluwer, 1998).

Tempting, but wrong (p. 71): the argument here was originally developed and published by H. L. A. Hart in 1961. It is now available in H. L. A. Hart, *The Concept of Law*, 3rd edn (Oxford: Clarendon, 2012), pp. 75–6.

when they drew up the constitution (p. 74): see Anthony King, *The Founding Father v. the People* (Cambridge, MA: Harvard University Press, 2012), ch. 2.

Consider just one example in Arizona (p. 79): for this example, see Christopher A. Coury, 'Direct Democracy through Initiative and Referendum: Checking the Balance', *Notre Dame Journal of Law, Ethics and Public Policy* 8.2 (2014), available at http://scholarship.law.nd.edu/ndjlepp/vol8/iss2/7 and at https://scholarship.law.nd.edu/cgi/viewcontent.cgi?article=1446&context=ndjlepp (accessed 7 January 2018) I thank Alan Ware for this reference.

what is known as the jury theorem (p. 83): there is an excellent summary of modern scholarship on the jury theorem in Robert E. Goodin, *Reflective Democracy* (Oxford: Oxford University Press, 2003), ch. 5. The original theorem was formulated by the Marquis de Condorcet.

plural voices (p. 100): I take from John Rawls, *Political Liberalism* (New York: Columbia University Press, 1996) the idea that plural voices are the predictable consequence of human reasoning working under free institutions. The more one thinks about it, the more profound a significance this idea seems to have.

Referendums take different forms (p. 107): a good discussion of this variety that is still worth reading can be found in Margaret Canovan, *Populism* (London: Junction Books, 1981), ch. 5.

the guardrails of democracy (p. 113): I take this phrase from Steven Levitsky and Daniel Ziblatt, *How Democracies Die* (New York: Penguin Random House, 2018), a thought-provoking study of how democracies die from within.

'Human kind cannot bear very much reality' (p. 114): 'Burnt Norton', in T. S. Eliot, *Four Quartets*, reprinted in *The Complete Poems and Plays of T. S. Eliot* (London: Faber & Faber, 1969), p. 172.